E S T A T E   P U B L I

BEDFORD

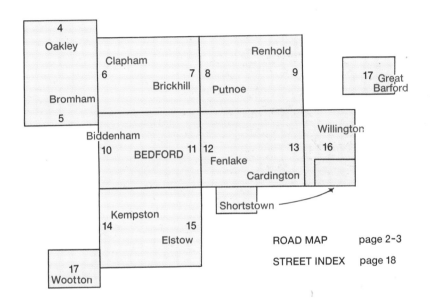

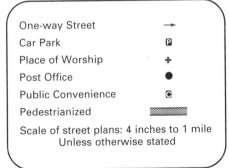

ROAD MAP	page 2-3
STREET INDEX	page 18

Every effort has been made to verify the accuracy of information in this book but the publishers cannot accept responsibility for expense or loss caused by any error or omission. Information that will be of assistance to the user of the maps will be welcomed.

The representation of a road, track or footpath on the maps in this atlas is no evidence of the existence of a right of way.

One-way Street	→
Car Park	Ⓟ
Place of Worship	✝
Post Office	●
Public Convenience	Ⓒ
Pedestrianized	▨

Scale of street plans: 4 inches to 1 mile
Unless otherwise stated

Street plans prepared and published by ESTATE PUBLICATIONS, Bridewell House, TENTERDEN, KENT, and based upon the ORDNANCE SURVEY mapping with the permission of The Controller of H. M. Stationery Office.

The publishers acknowledge the co-operation of the local authorities of towns represented in this atlas.

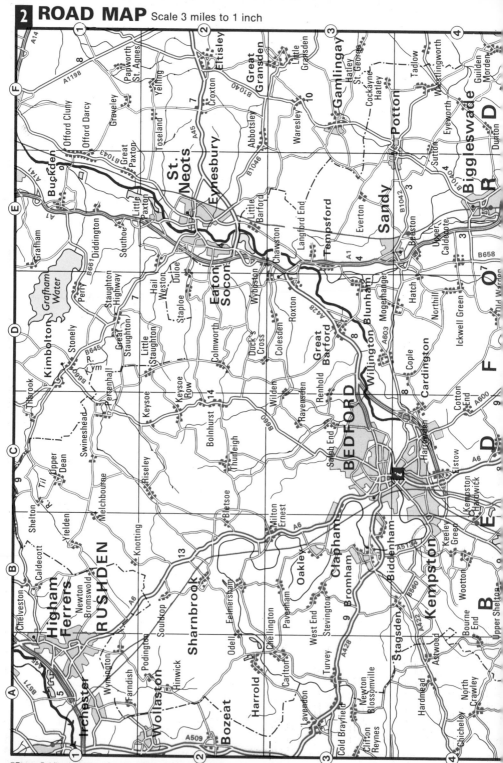

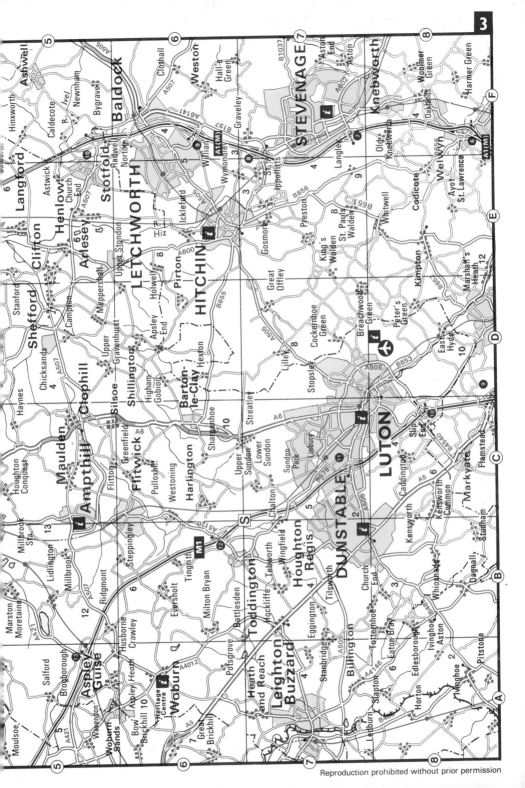

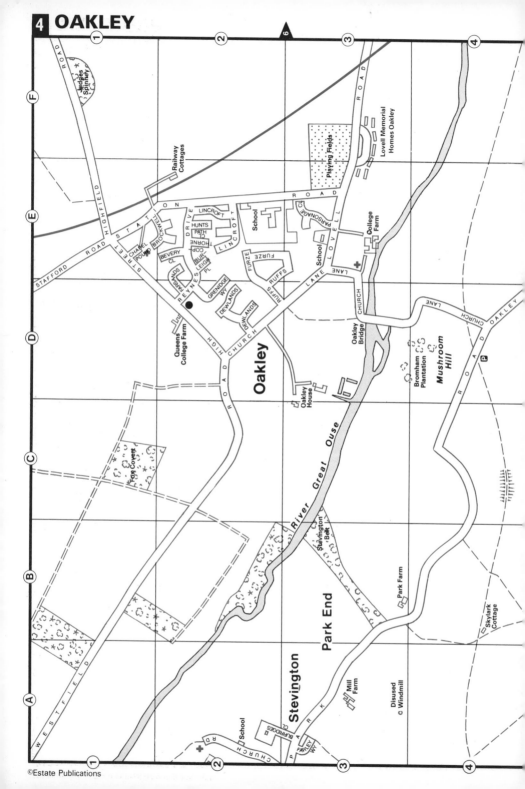

4 OAKLEY

Judges Spinney

Railway Cottages

Playing Fields

Lovell Memorial Homes Oakley

HIGHFIELD ROAD

STAFFORD ROAD

STATION STREET

CHAPEL POUND

BROXWELL

BEVERY CL

LINCROFT

HUNTS PATH

THORNE

COOP

BURLEIGH PL

School

ROAD

DRIVE

LINCROFT

FURZE

FURZE

RUFFS

PARSONAGE CL

School

LOVELL LANE

College Farm

REYNES

GRENIDGE WY

DEWLANDS

RUFFS LANE

CHURCH

Queens College Farm

DEWLANDS

HIGH ROAD

CHURCH ROAD

Oakley

Oakley Bridge

CHURCH LANE

OAKLEY ROAD

Bromham Plantation

Mushroom Hill

Oakley House

River Great Ouse

Fogs Covert

Stevington Belt

Park Farm

Skylark Cottage

Stevington

Park End

PARK

Mill Farm

Disused Windmill

School

BURRIDGES CL

FARR WY

CHURCH RD

WESTFIELD

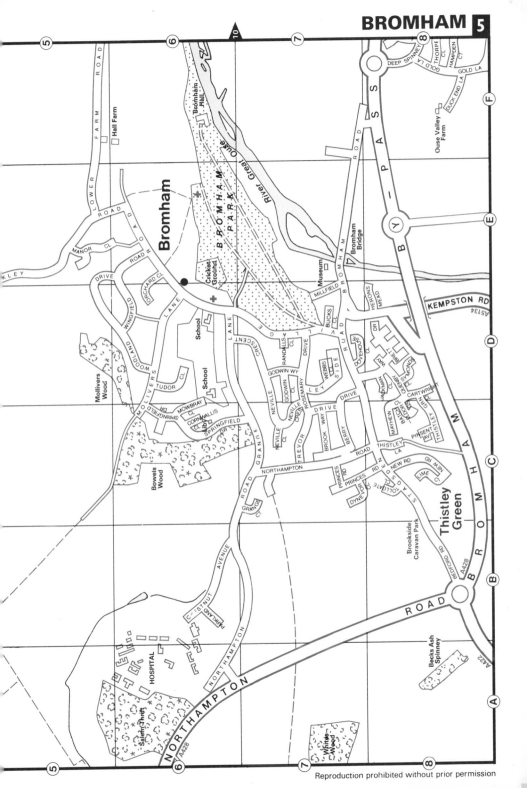

Hall Farm

Bromham Hall

Bromham

BROMHAM PARK

River Great Ouse

DEEP SPINNEY

THORPE
HAMPDEN CT
GOLD LA
GOLD LA
BUCK END LA

Ouse Valley Farm

BY-PASS

Bromham Bridge

Museum

Bromham Bridge

KEMPSTON RD
A5134

MILLFIELD

HERONS MEAD

BUCKS

Cricket Ground

School

School

Mollivers Wood

WINGFIELD
ORCHARD CL
ROAD
DRIVE
MANOR CL
LANE
TUDOR CL
WOODLAND
SPRINGFIELD
OLIVERS DR

RANDALLS
GODWIN WY
NEVILLE
GODWIN CL
NEVILLE CRES
ROSEMARY
WEBBS CL
CRESCENT
DRIVE
LEY
SIDE
ROAD
DOVEHOUSE

Bowels Wood

MOWBRAY CL
CORNWALLIS

NEVILLE CL
TREVOR
BROOK WAY
BERRY DRIVE
WAY
NORTHAMPTON ROAD

GRANGE ROAD
GRANGE CT

PRINCES
PRINCES RD
DYNSK
TOLLGATE
RD
STA
NEW RD
NEW RD
LIME
THISTLE LA
PINSENT LEY
THISTLEY AV

HACKMAN CL
BAGOT CL
QUEBEC
SY-MONDS
CARTWRIGHT
MAYHEW
BACON
BLOOR

Thistley Green

BEDFORD RD
Brookside Caravan Park

CHESTNUT CL
PARKLAND

HOSPITAL

Salem Thrift

NORTHAMPTON
A428

BROMHAM ROAD

Becks Ash Spinney

A422

Whites Wood

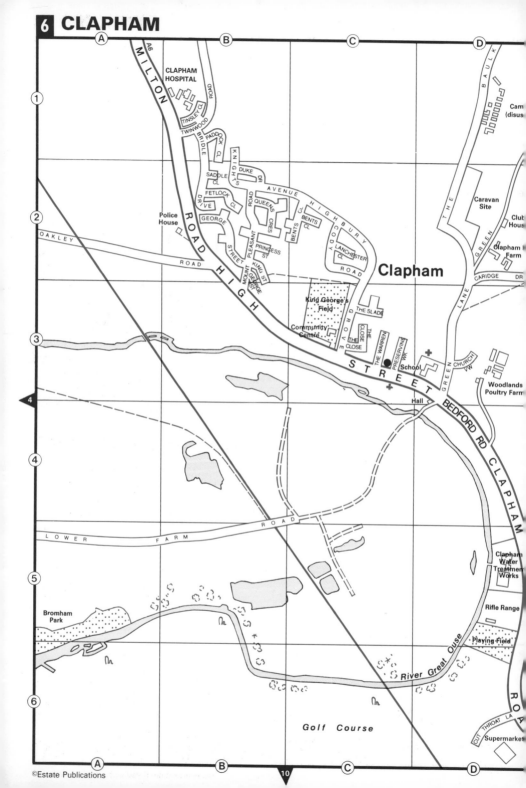

CLAPHAM HOSPITAL

MILTON

A6

TINSLE CL

TWINWOOD

BRIDLE

PADDOCK CL

KNIGHT'S

SADDLE CL

DUKE DR

FETLOCK CL

AVENUE

GEORGE

ROAD

QUEENS

CRES

BENTS CL

BENTS CL

HIGHBURY

Police House

DRIVE

MOUNT PLEASANT

STREET

PRINCESS ST

KING ST

KING GEORGE

COODY

LANCHESTER CL

ROAD

HIGH

ROAD

OAKLEY

ROAD

Clapham

King George's Field

THE SLADE

Community Centre

GROVE

THE CLOSE

THE WARREN

THE CLOSE

PRESERVINE WK

School

STREET

GREEN LANE

CHURCH

VW

Woodlands Poultry Farm

BEDFORD RD

CLAPHAM

Hall

BAULK

Cam (disus)

THE GREEN

Caravan Site

Club House

Clapham Farm

CARIDGE DR

LOWER

FARM

ROAD

Clapham Water Treatment Works

Rifle Range

Bromham Park

Playing Field

River Great Ouse

CUT THROAT LA

Supermarket

ROAD

Golf Course

©Estate Publications

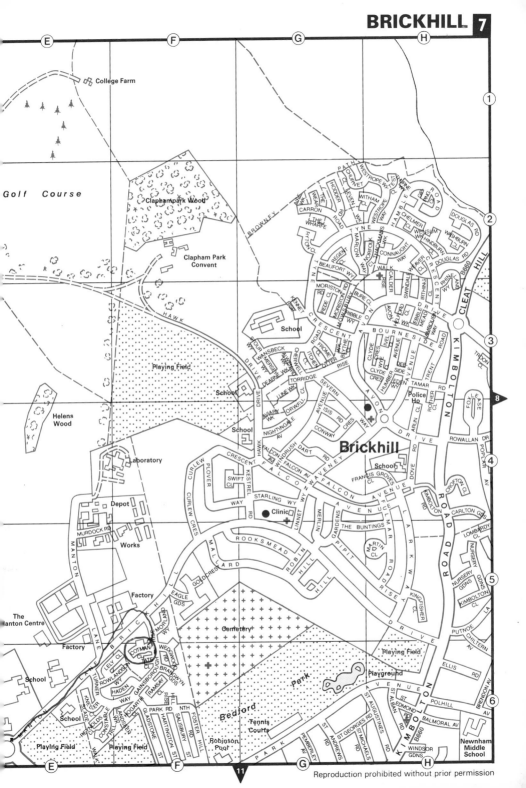

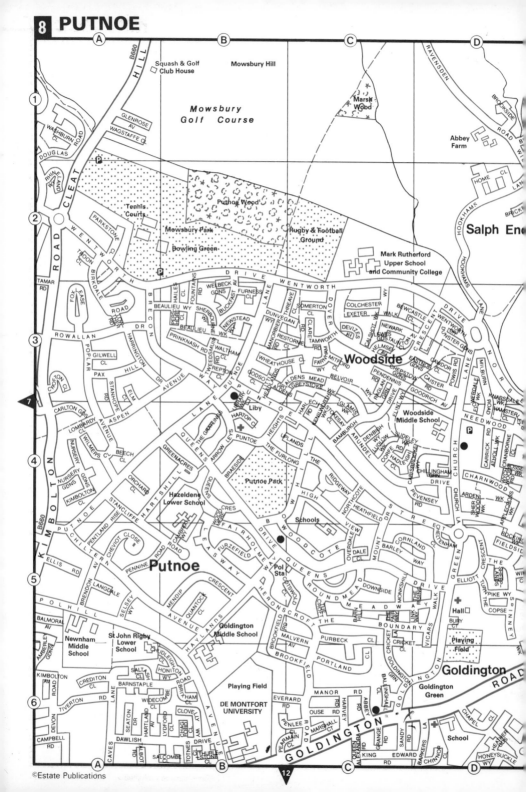

Mowsbury Hill

Squash & Golf
Club House

*Mowsbury
Golf Course*

Marsh
Wood

Abbey
Farm

Salph End

Putnoe Wood

Tennis
Courts

Mowsbury Park

Bowling Green

Rugby & Football
Ground

Mark Rutherford
Upper School
and Community College

Woodside

Liby

Woodside
Middle School

Putnoe Park

Hazeldene
Lower School

Schools

Putnoe

Pol
Sta

Hall

Playing
Field

Newnham
Middle
School

St John Rigby
Lower
School

Goldington
Middle School

Cricket

Goldington

Goldington
Green

Goldington
School

Playing Field

DE MONTFORT
UNIVERSITY

12

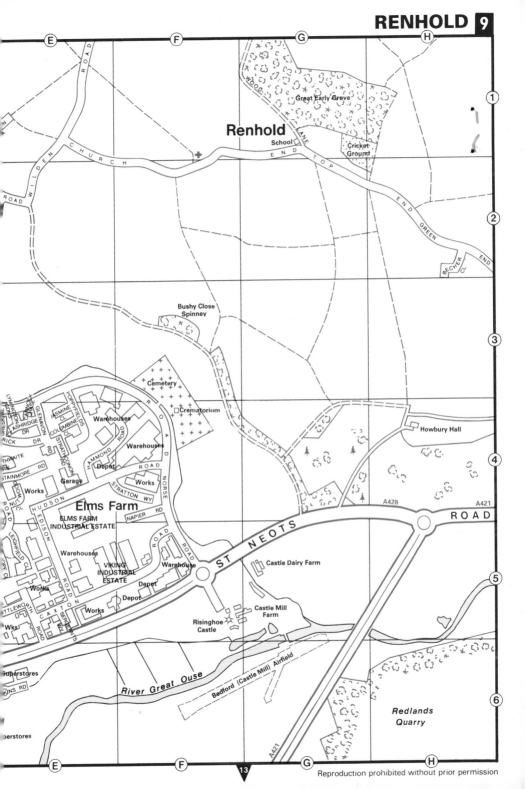

E F G H

1

Great Early Grove

Renhold

School

Cricket Ground

WILDEN ROAD

CHURCH ROAD

WOOD LANE

END

TOP END

GREEN END

BECKER CL

2

Bushy Close Spinney

3

Cemetery

Crematorium

Howbury Hall

LYMINGTON

ASHRIDGE DR

GLENAVON CL

HOPPYFIELDS CL

JASMINE CL

COLUMBINE CL

STRATTON COMN

HAMMOND ROAD

Warehouses

Warehouses

Depot

ROAD

NORSE ROAD

STAINMORE RD

RICK DR

Garage

Works

Works

A428

A421

4

Elms Farm

HUDSON ROAD

STRATTON WY

NAPIER RD

ELMS FARM INDUSTRIAL ESTATE

EDISON

LEIGHFIELD CL

ROAD

ROAD

ROAD

ST NEOTS

ROAD

Castle Dairy Farm

5

Warehouses

VIKING INDUSTRIAL ESTATE

Warehouse

Depot

Depot

Works

Superstores

CAXTON ROAD

SERGEANTS

Wks

Castle Mill Farm

Risinghoe Castle

6

River Great Ouse

Bedford (Castle Mill) Airfield

Redlands Quarry

A421

Superstores

E F G H

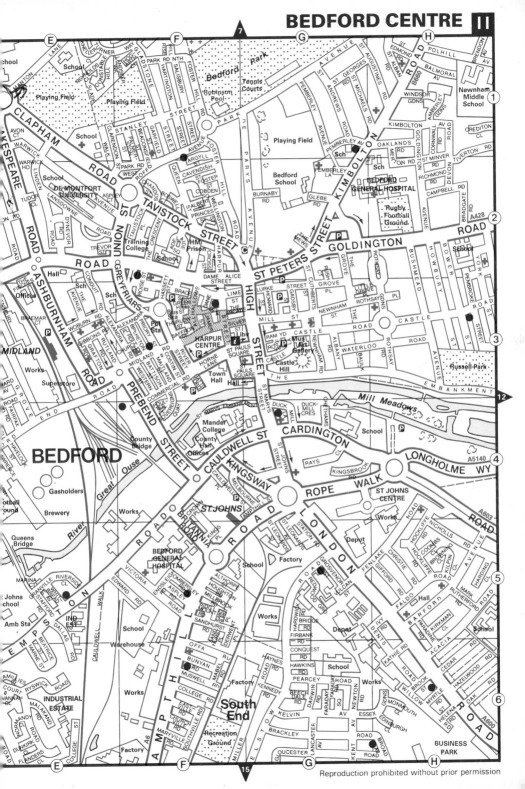

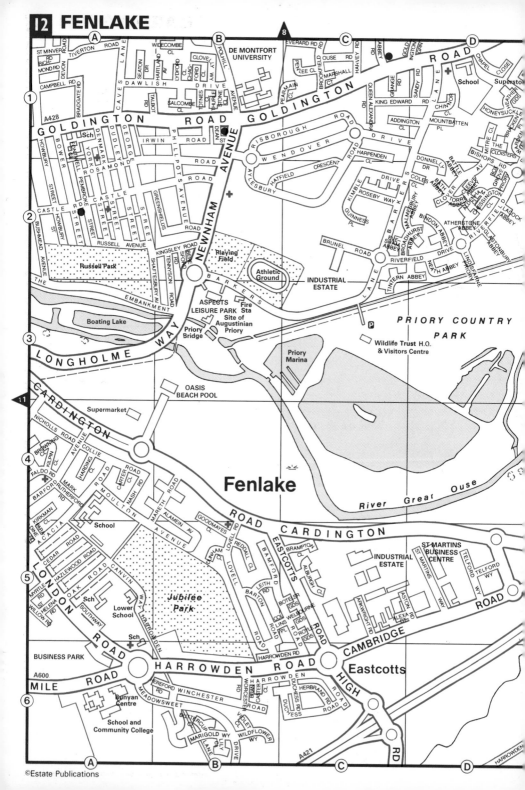

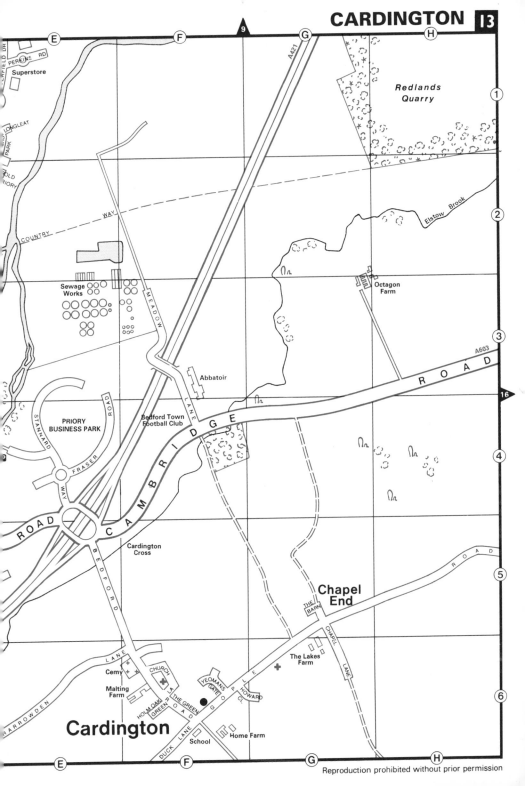

9

E · F · G · H

Superstore

PERKINS RD

CLAPFIELD DR

LONGLEAT PARK

OLD PRIORY

COUNTRY WAY

Redlands Quarry

Elstow Brook

1

2

Sewage Works

MEADOW

Octagon Farm

LANE

Abbatoir

A421

A603

ROAD

3

16

STANNARD ROAD

PRIORY BUSINESS PARK

Bedford Town Football Club

CAMBRIDGE

4

FRASER WAY

ROAD

ROAD

5

Cardington Cross

BEDFORD ROAD

Chapel End

THE BARN

CHAPEL LANE

The Lakes Farm

HARROWDEN LANE

LANE

Cemy

CHURCH LA

Malting Farm

HOLM OAK GREEN

THE GREEN

YEOMANS GATE

J. E. HOWARD CL

G O O

●

6

Cardington

DUCK LANE

School

Home Farm

E · F · G · H

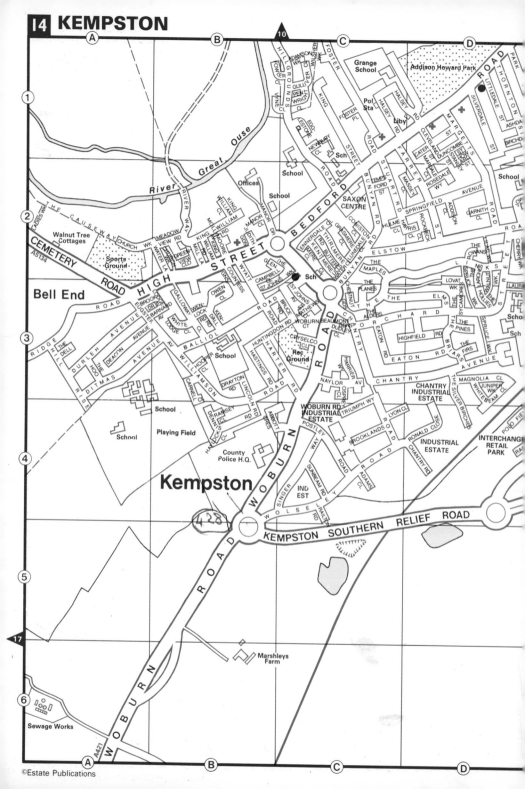

14 KEMPSTON

Kempston

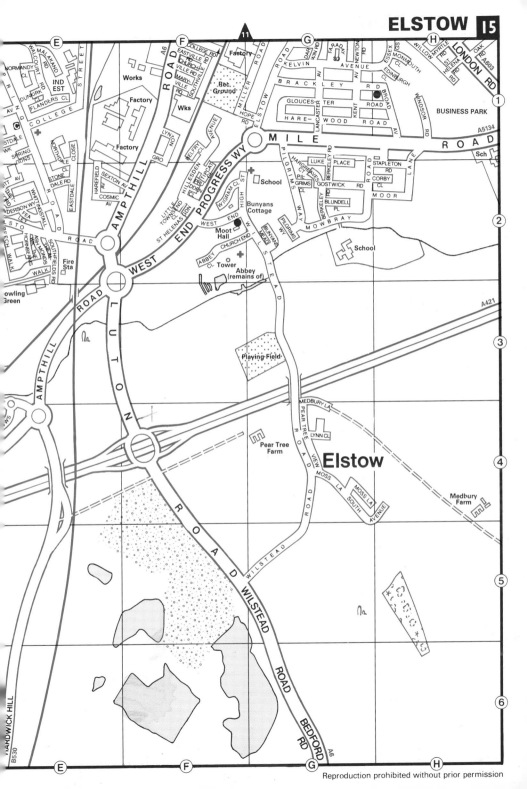

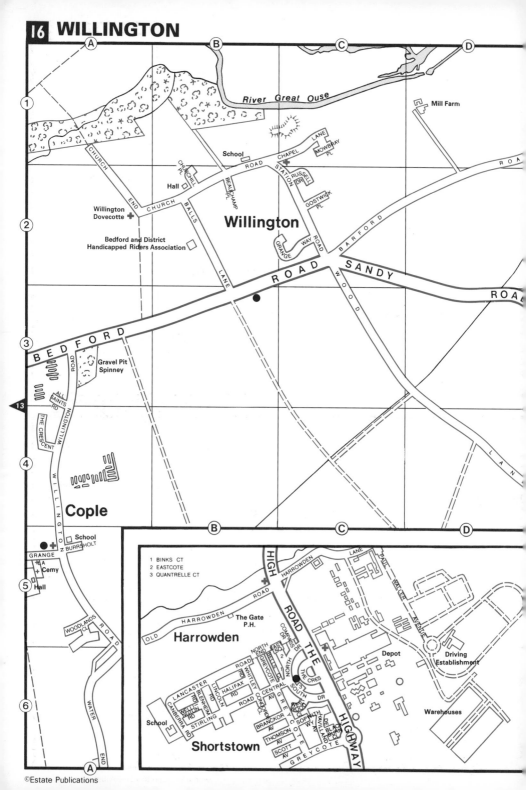

River Great Ouse

Mill Farm

School

CHAPEL LANE

MOWBRAY PL

STATION

RUSSEL DR

GOSTWICK PL

CHURCHILL

Hall

BEAUCHAMP PL

CHURCH END

CHURCH

BALLS

Willington Dovecotte

Willington

Bedford and District
Handicapped Riders Association

GRANGE

WAY

ROAD

ROAD

SANDY

ROAD

BARFORD

WOOD

ROAD

LANE

BEDFORD

ROAD

Gravel Pit
Spinney

ALL SAINTS RD

WILLINGTON RD

THE CRESCENT

13

Cople

School

BURRSHOLT

GRANGE

Cemy

Hall

WOODLANDS CL

ROAD

WATER END

LANE

1 BINKS CT
2 EASTCOTE
3 QUANTRELLE CT

HIGH

HARROWDEN

LANE

PAUL

WALSH

AVENUE

ROAD

THE

Harrowden

The Gate
P.H.

OLD

HARROWDEN

ROAD

COMPASS DR

NORTH END

GREYCOTE

WHITLEY ROAD

LANCASTER

BLENHEIM

WELLINGTON RD

LINCOLN

HALIFAX RD

CANBERRA RD

STIRLING

BRANCKER AV

THOMSON AV

SCOTT

CENTRAL AV

WESTWOOD

SOPWITH WY

HAVILLAND

DELAND

BLACK

GREYCOTE

THE CRES

SOUTH

THE

DR

HIGHWAY

Depot

Driving
Establishment

Warehouses

School

Shortstown

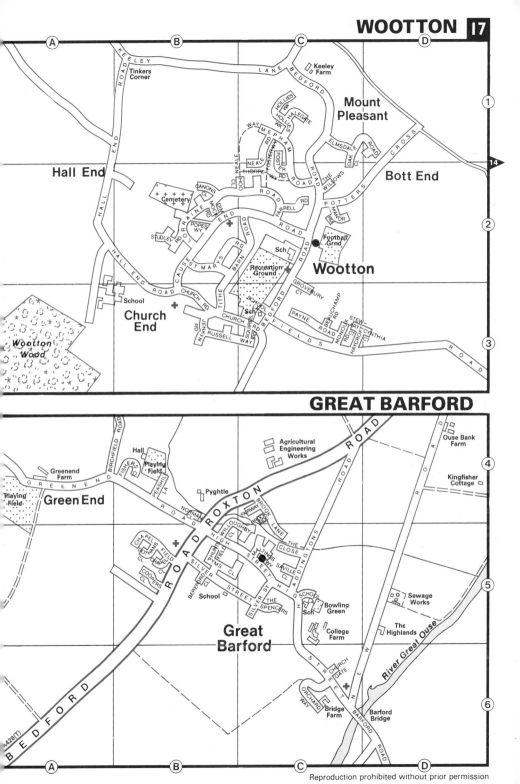

Hall End

Church End

Wootton Wood

Mount Pleasant

Bott End

Wootton

Tinkers Corner

Keeley Farm

Cemetery

School

School

Recreation Ground

Football Grnd

GREAT BARFORD

Greenend Farm

Hall

Playing Field

Green End

Playing Field

Pyghtle

Agricultural Engineering Works

Ouse Bank Farm

Kingfisher Cottage

School

School

Great Barford

Bowling Green

College Farm

Sewage Works

The Highlands

River Great Ouse

Church Gate

Bridge Farm

Barford Bridge

A - Z INDEX TO STREETS
with Postcodes

The Index includes some names for which there is insufficient space on the maps. These names are preceded by an * and are followed by the nearest adjoining thoroughfare.

BEDFORD

Abbey Clo. MK42 15 F2
Abbey Rd. MK41 8 C6
Abbott Cres. MK42 14 B4
Acacia Rd. MK42 11 H6
Adams Clo. MK42 14 C4
Adamson Wk. MK42 10 C6
Addington Clo. MK41 12 C1
Addingtons Rd. MK44 17 C4
Addison Clo. MK42 14 D2
Adelaide Sq. MK41 11 F2
Aire Wk. MK41 7 G2
Alamein Av. MK42 12 B4
Albany Rd. MK40 11 G3
Albert St. MK40 11 F2
Alburgh Clo. MK42 12 C5
Aldenham Clo. MK41 12 D2
Alexa Ct. MK42 12 C5
Alexandra Pl. MK40 11 F3
Alexandra Rd. MK40 11 E3
All Saints Rd. MK40 10 D3
All Saints Rd. MK44 16 A3
Allen Clo. MK40 10 D4
Allhallows. MK40 11 F3
Althorpe St. MK42 11 F5
Alwen Wk. MK41 7 G3
Amberley Gdns. MK40 11 H1
Ampthill Rd. MK42 11 F6
Ampthill St. MK42 11 G4
Applecross Wk. MK41 8 D4
Arden Wk. MK41 8 D4
Argyll St. MK40 11 F1
Arkwright Rd. MK42 12 C5
Arrow Leys. MK41 8 B4
Arun Clo. MK41 7 H4
Arundel Dri. MK41 7 H4
Ash Wk. MK42 15 E2
Ashburnham Rd. MK40 11 E2
Ashdale Av. MK42 14 D1
Ashridge Dri. MK41 9 E4
Aspects Leisure Pk. MK41 12 B3
Aspen Av. MK41 8 A4
Aspley Ct. MK40 11 E2
Aspley Rd. MK42 11 F5
Aston Rd. MK42 12 B5
Atholl Wk. MK41 8 D4
Aviary Wk. MK41 7 G4
Avon Ct. MK40 11 E1
Avon Dri. MK41 7 H4
Avon Wk. MK41 7 H3
Aylesbury Rd. MK41 12 B2

Ballinghall Clo. MK41 8 C6
Balliol Rd. MK42 14 B3
Balls La. MK44 16 B2
Balmoral Av. MK41 11 H1
*Balsall St East,
  Harpur St. MK40 11 F2
*Balsall St West,
  Harpur St. MK40 11 F2
Bamford Rd. MK42 12 B3
Barford Av. MK42 11 H5
Barford Rd,
  Great Barford. MK44 17 C5
Barford Rd,
  Willington. MK44 16 C2
Barkers La. MK41 12 B2
Barley Way. MK41 8 C5
Barnard Av. MK42 14 A3
Barnhill. MK41 8 C5
Barnstaple Rd. MK40 8 A6
Barton Rd. MK42 12 B5
Batcheldor Gdns. MK43 5 C8
Bath Abbey. MK41 12 D2
Battison St. MK40 11 F3
Battle Abbey. MK41 12 D2
Batts Ford. MK40 11 F1
Beaconsfield St. MK41 11 F1
Beatrice St. MK41 11 E5
Beauchamp Pl. MK44 16 B2
Beauchamp Rd. MK44 17 C3
Beaufort Way. MK41 7 G2
Beaulieu Wk. MK41 8 B3
Beaulieu Way. MK41 8 B3
Beaumont Gdns. MK42 14 C3
Becher Clo. MK41 9 H2
*Beckett St,
  Hassett St. MK40 11 F3

*Bedesman La,
  Duck Mill La. MK42 11 G4
Bedford Rd,
  Bromham. MK43 5 B8
Bedford Rd,
  Cardington. MK44 13 E4
Bedford Rd,
  Clapham. MK41 6 D4
Bedford Rd,
  Elstow. MK42 15 G6
Bedford Rd,
  Great Barford. MK44 17 A6
Bedford Rd,
  Kempston. MK42 14 C2
Bedford Rd,
  Willington. MK44 16 A3
Bedford Rd,
  Wootton. MK43 17 C1
Beech Clo. MK41 8 A4
*Beech Ct,
  Beech Rd. MK40 14 D2
Beech Dale Rd. MK42 11 G6
Beech Wk. MK42 15 E2
Belfry Clo. MK42 15 F1
Bells Clo. MK42 Inset 16
Belvoir Wk. MK41 8 C3
Bents Clo. MK41 6 C2
Bereford Clo. MK44 17 B5
Beresford Rd. MK40 12 B2
Berkeley Rd. MK41 15 G2
Berry Dri. MK43 5 C7
Beverley Cres. MK40 10 D2
Beverley Gro. MK40 10 D2
Bevery Clo. MK43 4 E2
Bewcastle Clo. MK41 8 C3
Biddenham Turn. MK40 10 B3
Bindon Abbey. MK41 12 D2
Binks Ct. MK42 Inset 16
Birichdale Av. MK41 14 D1
Birchfield Rd. MK44 17 A4
Birkdale Rd. MK41 8 A2
Birse Grn. MK41 12 D1
Bishops Rd. MK41 12 D1
Blackburn Clo. MK42 Inset 16
Blenheim Rd. MK42 Inset 16
Blundell Pl. MK42 15 G2
Blythe Clo. MK41 7 G3
Boswell Ct. MK40 11 F2
Botoler Gdns. MK42 12 C5
Bourneside. MK41 7 H3
Bower St. MK40 12 A1
Bowhill. MK41 8 B4
Boxgrove Priory. MK41 12 D2
Boyde Gdns. MK40 10 D4
Brace St. MK40 11 F3
Bracken Pl. MK41 12 D1
Brackley Rd. MK42 15 G1
Bradgate Rd. MK40 11 H2
Braemar Ct. MK41 11 E3
Braeside. MK41 8 B4
Brampton Clo. MK42 12 C5
Brancaster Clo. MK42 12 B6
Brangwyn Gdns. MK41 7 H6
Branckor Av. MK42 Inset 16
Brecon Way. MK41 8 A3
Brendon Av. MK41 8 A5
Brereton Rd. MK41 11 F3
Brett Dri. MK43 5 D8
Brickfield Rd. MK41 8 D2
Brickhill Dri. MK41 7 F5
Bridge Rd. MK42 11 G5
Bridle Dri. MK41 6 B1
Britannia Rd. MK42 11 F4
Brixham Clo. MK42 8 B6
Broad Av. MK41 15 H1
Broadhurst Abbey. MK41 12 C2
Brockwell. MK43 4 E1
Bromham By-Pass. MK43 5 B8
Bromham Rd,
  Bedford. MK40 10 D2
Bromham Rd,
  Biddenham. MK40 10 A2
Bromham Rd,
  Bromham. MK43 5 D7
Brook Dri. MK41 14 A3
Brook La. MK44 17 C4
Brook St. MK42 11 H6
Brook Way. MK41 5 C7
Brookfield Rd. MK41 8 B5
Brooklands. MK42 14 A4
Brookside. MK44 17 C4
Brookside. MK41 8 D1
Browney Path. MK41 7 G2
Browning Clo. MK41 11 H5
Bruce Rd. MK42 14 C3
Brunel Rd. MK41 12 C2
Bruthwaite Grn. MK41 9 E4
Buckfast Av. MK41 8 B3
Bucks Clo. MK43 5 D7

Bunyan Rd,
  South End. MK42 11 F6
Bunyan Rd,
  Kempston. MK42 14 C2
Bunyans Mead. MK42 15 G2
Bure Clo. MK41 7 G3
Burgess Clo. MK42 10 B5
Burleigh Pl. MK43 4 E2
Burnaby Rd. MK40 11 G2
Burridges Clo. MK43 4 A3
Burrsholt. MK43 16 A5
Bury Ct. MK41 8 D5
Bury Wk. MK41 8 D6
Bushmead Av. MK40 11 H2
Butler Way. MK41 10 C6
Buttercup Clo. MK42 12 B6
Buttermere Clo. MK41 14 C2
Byron Cres. MK40 10 D1

Caister Rd. MK41 8 D3
Calder Rise. MK41 7 H2
Calshot Wk. MK41 8 C3
Cambrian Way. MK41 8 B5
Cambridge Rd. MK42 12 C6
Campbell Clo. MK42 14 B2
Campbell Rd. MK40 11 H2
Canberra Rd. MK42 Inset 16
Cannock Chase. MK41 9 E4
Canons Clo. MK43 17 B2
Canterbury Clo. MK42 10 D5
Canvin Way. MK42 12 A5
Cardington Rd. MK44 11 G4
Caridge Dri. MK42 6 D2
Carisbrooke Way. MK41 8 C4
Carlisle Rd. MK40 10 C4
Carlton Gdns. MK41 8 A4
Carnell Clo. MK42 14 B3
Carrick Rd. MK41 8 D4
Carron Rd. MK41 7 G2
Carter Clo. MK42 12 A4
Cartwright Clo. MK43 5 D8
Castle La. MK41 11 G3
Castle Rd. MK40 11 G3
Cater St. MK42 14 D1
Cauldwell Pl. MK41 11 F4
Cauldwell St. MK42 11 F4
Cauldwell Wk. MK41 11 E6
Cause End Rd. MK43 17 B2
*Cavendish Ct, Shakespeare
  Rd. MK40 11 E1
Cavendish St. MK40 11 F2
Caves La. MK40 12 A1
Cawdor Clo. MK41 8 D3
Caxton Rd. MK41 9 E5
Cedar Rd. MK42 11 H6
Cemetery Rd. MK43 14 A2
Central Av. MK42 Inset 16
Chagford Clo. MK40 8 B6
Chander Path. MK42 10 B6
Chandos St. MK41 11 F2
Chantry Av. MK41 14 C3
Chantry Ind Est. MK42 14 D3
Chantry Rd. MK41 14 C3
Chapel Clo. MK41 12 D1
Chapel Clo. MK44 17 B5
Chapel Field. MK44 17 B5
Chapel La,
  Cardington. MK44 13 G5
Chapel La,
  Willington. MK44 16 C1
Chapel Pound. MK43 4 E1
Chapman Clo. MK40 10 B5
Charnwood Av. MK41 8 A5
Chaucer Rd. MK40 11 E2
Chelmer Rd. MK41 7 H2
Cheltenham Clo. MK41 8 D5
Chepstow Gdns. MK41 8 D5
Cherry Wk. MK42 14 D2
Cherwell Rd. MK41 7 G3
Chessington Clo. MK41 12 D2
Chester Rd. MK40 10 C4
Chesterton Mews. MK40 10 D2
Chestnut Av. MK43 5 B6
Chestnut Clo. MK40 10 D3
Chestnut Gdns. MK41 11 G4
Chethams. MK42 11 G4
Cheviot Clo. MK41 8 A5
Chillingham Grn. MK41 8 D4
Chiltern Av. MK41 8 A5
Chinnor Clo. MK42 12 D1
Christie Rd. MK42 11 H5
Chudleigh Clo. MK40 8 B6
Church End. MK42 10 A3
Church End. MK42 11 E6
Church End. MK41 9 E1
Church End. MK44 16 A1
Church Gate. MK44 17 C5
Church La. MK41 8 D4
Church La. MK43 4 D2
Church La. MK41 8 D4

Church Rd,
  Church End. MK43 17 B3
Church Rd,
  Stevington. MK43 4 A2
Church Rd,
  Willington. MK44 16 A1
Church St. MK40 11 F3
*Church Sq,
  Allhallows. MK40 11 F3
Church View. MK41 6 D3
Church Wk. MK42 14 A2
Churchill Pl. MK44 16 B2
Churchville Rd. MK42 11 F6
Churnet Clo. MK41 7 G2
Clapham Rd,
  Bedford. MK41 11 E1
Clapham Rd,
  Clapham. MK41 6 D4
Clare Rd. MK40 8 C3
Clarendon St. MK41 11 E1
Cleat Hill. MK41 8 A1
Cleeve Abbey. MK41 12 D2
Cleveland St. MK41 14 D1
Clipstone Clo. MK41 9 E4
Clovelly Way. MK40 8 B6
Clover Av. MK41 12 D2
Clyde Cres. MK41 7 H3
Cobden Sq. MK40 11 F2
Cody Rd. MK41 6 C2
Colchester Way. MK41 8 C3
Coles Clo. MK41 12 D2
College Rd. MK42 11 F6
College St. MK42 15 E1
Collie Rd. MK42 12 A4
Collins Pl. MK42 12 B5
Columbine Clo. MK41 9 E4
Commercial Rd. MK40 11 F3
Compass Dri. MK42 Inset 16
Concorde Clo. MK42 Inset 16
Conduit Rd. MK40 11 E2
Coniston Clo. MK42 14 C2
Connaught Way. MK41 7 H2
Conquest Rd. MK42 11 G6
Constable Hill. MK41 7 E6
Conway Cres. MK41 7 G4
Coombs Clo. MK42 11 H5
Coopers Clo. MK44 17 B5
Cople Rd. MK44 13 F6
Copthorne Clo. MK43 4 E2
Corby Clo. MK42 15 H2
Corfe Rd. MK41 8 C4
Corland. MK41 8 C5
Cornwall Rd. MK40 11 H1
Cornwallis Clo. MK43 5 C6
Cosmic Av. MK42 15 E2
Costin St. MK40 11 F3
Cotman Clo. MK41 7 F6
Cotswold Clo. MK41 8 C5
Country Way. MK44 13 E2
Coventry Rd. MK40 10 D3
Cowper Rd. MK40 11 G1
Coxs Clo. MK40 10 D4
Cranborne Clo. MK41 8 D4
Crediton Clo. MK40 8 A6
Cricket Clo. MK41 8 C5
Cricket La. MK41 8 C6
Crofton Clo. MK41 8 A3
Cromwell Rd. MK41 11 E4
Cross St. MK40 11 F2
Crown Pl. MK42 11 F4
Cryselco Clo. MK41 14 C3
Curlew Cres. MK41 7 F4
Cut Throat La. MK41 6 D6
Cutcliffe Gdns. MK40 10 D3
Cutcliffe Gro. MK40 10 D3
Cutcliffe Pl. MK40 10 D3
Cynthia Ct. MK43 17 C3

Dale Clo. MK41 8 C5
Dallas Rd. MK42 11 E5
Dame Alice St. MK40 11 F2
Dane St. MK40 11 F3
Darlow Dri. MK40 10 B2
Dart Rd. MK41 7 G4
Darwin Rd. MK42 11 G6
Dawlish Dri. MK40 10 A3
Days La. MK40 10 B3
De Havilland Av.
  MK42 Inset 16
De Parys Av. MK40 11 G1
Deacon Clo. MK42 14 A3
Dean St. MK40 12 B1
Dearne Wk. MK41 7 G3
Deep Spinney. MK40 10 A3
Deeside. MK41 7 H3
Denbigh Way. MK41 8 B3
Denmark St. MK40 12 A1
Dennis Rd. MK42 14 B4
Denton Clo. MK42 10 B5

Dents Rd. MK42 11 H5
*Derby Pl,
  Tavistock St. MK40 11 F2
Derwent Pl. MK42 11 F5
Devizes Av. MK41 8 C3
Devon Rd. MK40 11 H2
Dewlands. MK43 4 D2
Dimmock Rd. MK43 17 B2
Ditmas Av. MK42 14 A3
Donnelly Dri. MK41 12 D1
Dothans Clo. MK44 17 B5
Douglas Rd. MK41 7 H2
Dove Rd. MK41 7 H4
Dovehouse Clo. MK43 5 D7
Dover Cres. MK41 8 C3
Downfield Way. MK42 10 C6
Downside. MK41 8 C5
Drayton Rd. MK42 14 B3
Duchess Rd. MK42 12 C6
Duck End La. MK40 10 A2
Duck La. MK44 13 F6
Duck Mill Cres. MK42 11 G4
Duck Mill La. MK42 11 G4
Dudley Clo. MK42 14 C3
Dudley St. MK40 12 A1
Duke Dri. MK41 6 B2
*Duke St,
  Mill St. MK40 11 G3
Duncombe St. MK42 14 D1
Dunham Clo. MK42 12 B5
Dunkirk Clo. MK42 11 E6
Dunster Gdns. MK41 8 D3
Dunvegan Way. MK41 8 B3
Dunville Rd. MK40 10 D3
Durler Av. MK41 14 A3
Dynevor Clo. MK43 5 C7
Dynevor Rd. MK41 11 E2

Eagle Gdns. MK41 7 F5
Earls Holme. MK42 10 B5
East Sq. MK42 Inset 16
Eastcote. MK41 Inset 16
Eastcotts Rd. MK42 12 B5
Eastdale Clo. MK42 15 E2
Eastnor Gdns. MK41 8 D3
Eastville Rd. MK42 11 F6
Eaton Rd. MK42 14 C3
Ebble Mead. MK41 7 H3
Eden Way. MK41 7 H3
Edinburgh Clo. MK41 11 H6
Edison Rd. MK41 9 E5
Edward Rd. MK42 11 E5
Egglestone Clo. MK42 14 C1
Elger Clo. MK40 10 C2
Elliott Cres. MK41 8 D5
Ellis Rd. MK41 8 A5
Elm Clo. MK41 8 A3
Elms Farm Ind Est.
  MK41 9 E4
Elmsdale Rd. MK43 17 C1
Elstow Rd,
  Kempston. MK42 14 C2
Elstow Rd,
  South End. MK42 11 G6
Ely Way. MK42 10 C5
Emmerton Rd. MK42 10 B6
Endsleigh Rd. MK41 11 F5
Ennerdale Clo. MK42 14 C2
Essex Gdns. MK41 11 G6
Ettrick Dri. MK41 9 E4
Eugster Av. MK42 14 A3
Everard Rd. MK41 8 B6
Evesham Abbey. MK41 12 C2
Exeter Way. MK41 8 C3

Fairfax Rd. MK40 11 E4
Fairholme. MK41 8 B5
Fairway. MK44 17 C4
Falcon Av. MK41 7 G4
Faldo Rd. MK42 11 H5
Faraday Rd. MK40 11 G6
Faraday Sq. MK41 11 G6
Farley Way. MK41 4 A3
Farnham Rd. MK41 8 C3
Farrell Rd. MK41 17 C2
Farrer St. MK42 14 C1
Farsands. MK43 4 D2
Fearnley Cres. MK42 15 E2
Fenlake Rd. MK42 11 G5
*Fernlea Clo,
  Ousleand Rd. MK40 10 D4
Fetlock Clo. MK42 6 B2
Fields Rd. MK43 17 C3
Fieldside. MK41 8 D5
Firbank Rd. MK42 11 G5
Fisher Clo. MK44 17 C4
Fishers Clo. MK41 11 E6
Fleming Clo. MK40 10 A2
Flint Way. MK41 11 F5
Flowerdale Wk. MK41 8 D4

Fontwell Clo. MK40 12 A1
Ford End Rd. MK40 10 D4
Foster Hill Rd. MK41 11 F1
Foster Pl. MK42 14 C1
Foster Rd. MK42 17 C1
Foster St. MK40 11 F2
Fosterway. MK42 17 C2
Fountain Gro. MK42 10 C6
Fountains Rd. MK41 8 B3
Fowler Clo. MK42 10 B6
Foxgloves. MK40 10 D2
Foxlease. MK41 8 A3
Francis Groves Clo. MK41 7 G4
Franklyn Gdns. MK40 10 A2
Fraser Rd. MK44 13 E4
Frome Clo. MK41 7 G3
Fulmar Rd. MK41 7 H4
Furness Clo. MK41 8 B3
Furzefield. MK41 8 B5

Gadsby St. MK40 11 G3
Gainsborough Rise. MK41 7 F5
Galloway Clo. MK42 14 B3
Garden Clo. MK42 10 C6
Gardener Pl. MK40 10 A2
Garfield Clo. MK41 11 F1
Garnith Clo. MK42 14 D2
George St. MK41 6 B2
George St. MK40 12 A1
Gibbons Rd. MK40 11 E3
Gifford Rd. MK41 11 H5
Gilbert Clo. MK42 10 B5
Gilwell Clo. MK41 8 A3
Gipping Clo. MK41 7 H2
Gladstone St. MK41 7 F6
Glamis Wk. MK41 8 C4
Glastonbury Abbey. MK41 12 D2
Glebe Rd. MK40 11 G2
Glenavon Clo. MK41 9 E4
Glenrose Av. MK41 8 A1
Gloucester Rd. MK42 15 G1
Godso Clo. MK41 8 B3
Godwin Clo. MK43 5 D7
Godwin Way. MK43 5 D7
Gold La. MK40 10 A2
Goldcrest. MK42 7 F5
Goldington Av. MK40 11 H1
Goldington Grn. MK41 8 C6
Goldington Rd. MK40 11 G2
Goodmayes Clo. MK42 .12 B4
Goodrich Av. MK41 8 D3
Gostwick Pl. MK44 16 C2
Gostwick Rd. MK42 15 G2
Gower Dri. MK40 10 B2
Grafton Rd. MK40 11 E3
*Granad St,
  Lurke St. MK40 11 G3
Granet Clo. MK40 10 D2
Grange Ct. MK43 5 C7
Grange La. MK43 5 C7
Grange La. MK44 16 A5
Grange Rd. MK41 12 C1
Grange Way. MK44 16 C2
Granville St. MK42 11 E5
Grasmere Clo. MK42 14 C2
Gratton Rd. MK40 10 D3
Great Aldens. MK41 8 B3
Green Hill St. MK41 9 H2
Green Hill St. MK40 11 F3
Green La,
  Clapham. MK41 6 D3
Green La,
  Renhold. MK41 9 E1
Green View Clo. MK42 14 B2
Greenacres. MK41 8 B4
Greenend Rd. MK44 17 A4
Greenshields Rd. MK42 12 A2
Grenidge Way. MK43 4 D2
Greskine Clo. MK41 9 E4
Greycote. MK42 Inset 16
Greyfrairs. MK42 11 F2
Greystoke Wk. MK41 8 C3
Grosvenor St. MK42 11 G5
Grove Pl. MK40 11 G3
Grovebury Ct. MK43 17 C2
Guinness Pl. MK41 2 C2
Gulliver Clo. MK42 10 C6
Gunnersbury Pk. MK41 13 E1

Haden Clo. MK41 7 F6
Hadleigh Clo. MK41 8 C4
Hailes Clo. MK41 8 B3
Halegate. MK43 17 C1
Halifax Rd. MK42 Inset 16
Hall End Rd. MK43 17 B1
Halsey Rd. MK41 14 C1
Hamble Rd. MK41 7 H2
Hammond Rd. MK41 9 E4
Hampden Ct. MK40 10 A2
Hamsterley Clo. MK41 8 D4
Harding Clo. MK42 11 H5
Hardwick Hill. MK42 15 E6
Hardwick Rd. MK42 11 G5
Harefield Av. MK42 15 E2

Harewood Rd. MK42 15 G1
Hargreaves Ct. MK42 15 G2
Harlech Rd. MK41 8 C4
Harold Priory. MK41 13 E2
Harpenden Clo. MK41 12 C1
Harpur St. MK40 11 F2
Harrier Way. MK42 14 C3
Harrington Dri. MK41 8 A3
Harris Clo. MK42 14 C2
Harrowden La,
  Cardington. MK44 13 E6
Harrowden La
  Eastcotts. MK42 12 A5
Harrowden La,
  Harrowden. MK42 Inset 16
Harrowden Rd. MK42 12 B6
Harter Rd. MK42 14 B3
Hartington St. MK41 7 F6
Hartland Av. MK40 8 A6
Hartop Clo. MK42 8 B4
Hartshill. MK41 8 A4
Hartwell Dri. MK42 10 C6
Harvey Rd. MK41 11 F3
Hassett St. MK40 11 F3
Hastings Rd. MK42 14 B3
Hatfield Cres. MK41 12 B2
Havelock St. MK40 11 E4
*Hawes Ct,
  Harpur St. MK40 11 F2
Hawk Dri. MK41 7 G4
Hawkins Rd. MK42 11 G6
Hawthorne Av. MK40 10 D4
Haycroft. MK43 17 C3
Haylands Way. MK41 8 B6
Haylock Clo. MK42 14 B4
Haynes Rd. MK41 11 G6
Hazelwood Rd. MK42 11 H6
Heather Gdns. MK41 12 D1
Heathfield. MK41 8 C4
Helford Clo. MK41 7 H3
Helmsey Av. MK41 8 C3
Henderson Way. MK41 15 E2
Herbrand Rd. MK42 12 C6
Hereford Rd. MK41 12 B6
Herons Mead. MK43 5 D8
Heronscroft. MK41 8 B5
Hickling Clo. MK41 10 C4
High Rd,
  Eastcotts. MK42 12 C6
High Rd,
  Harrowden. MK42 Inset 16
High St,
  Bedford. MK40 11 G3
High St,
  Clapham. MK41 6 B2
High St, Elstow. MK42 15 F2
High St,
  Great Barford. MK44 17 B5
High St,
  Kempston. MK42 14 A3
High St,Oakley. MK43 4 D2
High View. MK41 8 C4
Highbury Gro. MK41 6 C2
Highfield Rd. MK41 14 D3
Highfield Rd. MK43 4 E1
*Hilbre Grange, Shakespeare
  Rd. MK41 11 E1
Hill Rise. MK41 7 F6
Hill Rise. MK42 14 A3
Hillesden Av. MK41 15 F2
Hillgrounds Rd. MK42 10 B5
Hindburn Clo. MK41 7 H2
Hockliffe Rd. MK41 11 H5
Hodder Rd. MK41 7 G2
Hogarth Clo. MK41 7 F6
Holden Clo. MK40 10 A2
Hollies Wk. MK43 17 C1
Holm Oak Green. MK41 8 D2
Home Clo. MK41 8 D2
Honey Hill Gdns. MK40 10 D4
Honey Hill Rd. MK40 10 C4
Honeysuckle Way. MK41 10 D3
Honiton Way. MK40 8 B6
Hoo Clo. MK41 7 C2
Hookhams La. MK41 8 D2
Hooper Clo. MK41 14 B3
Hope Rd. MK42 15 F1
Horne La. MK40 11 F3
Houghton Rd. MK41 11 F5
Howard Av. MK40 11 E3
Howard Rd. MK44 13 F6
Howard Pl. MK41 11 E3
Howard Rd. MK41 11 G3
Howard St. MK40 14 D1
Howbury St. MK40 11 H2
Howden Gdns. MK40 10 B2
Hudson Rd. MK41 9 E4
Hulme Clo. MK42 14 C2
Humber Av. MK41 7 H3
Huntingdon Rd. MK42 14 B3
Hunts Field. MK44 17 B5
Hunts Path. MK42 4 E1
Hurst Gro. MK43 10 D3
Hurst Pl. MK42 11 F5
Iddesleigh Rd. MK40 10 D4

INDUSTRIAL ESTATES:
Aspects Leisure Pk.
  MK41 12 B3
Chantry Ind Est. MK42 14 D3
Elms Farm Ind Est.
  MK41 9 E4
Interchange Retail Pk.
  MK42 7 E5
Manton Centre. MK41 7 E5
Priory Business
  Centre. MK44 13 E4
St Martins Business
  Centre. MK42 12 D5
Viking Ind Est. MK42 9 E5
Woburn Rd Ind Est.
  MK42 14 C4
Irthing Clo. MK41 7 H3
Irwin Rd. MK42 12 A1
Isis Rd. MK41 7 G4
Ison Clo. MK40 10 B2
Itchen Clo. MK41 7 G3
Ivel Clo. MK41 7 H3
Ivy Rd. MK42 11 H5

Jacey Ct. MK42 10 B5
Jackman Clo. MK43 5 D8
James St. MK40 11 F3
Jasmine Clo. MK41 9 E4
Jenkyn Rd. MK43 17 B3
Johnson Clo. MK40 10 B2
Jowitt Av. MK42 14 D2
Judith Gdns. MK42 14 B2
Juniper Wk. MK42 14 D3

Kathie Rd. MK42 11 H6
Keats Clo. MK40 10 D1
Keeley La. MK43 17 B1
Kelvin Av. MK41 11 G6
Kempston Rd. MK42 11 E6
Kempston Rd. MK43 5 D8
Kempston Southern
  Relief Rd. MK42 14 B5
Kendall Rd. MK41 8 C4
Kenilworth Wk. MK41 8 C4
Kennedy Rd. MK42 11 G6
Kennet Rise. MK41 7 G3
Kent Av. MK42 15 G1
Kentmere Clo. MK41 14 C2
Kershope Clo. MK41 9 E5
Kestrel Rd. MK41 7 G4
*Kielder Path,
  Hamsterley Clo. MK41 8 D4
Kilpin Clo. MK41 11 H5
Kimble Dri. MK41 11 G2
Kimbolton Av. MK41 11 H1
Kimbolton Clo. MK41 11 G2
Kimbolton Rd. MK40 11 G2
Kimbolton Rd. MK41 7 H3
King Edward Rd. MK41 12 C1
King St. MK42 14 C1
King St. MK41 6 B2
King William Clo. MK42 14 B2
King William Rd. MK42 14 B2
Kingfisher Clo. MK41 7 H4
Kings Pl. MK42 7 H4
Kingsbrook Rd. MK41 11 G4
Kingsley Rd. MK40 12 B2
Kingsway. MK41 11 F4
Kirkman Clo. MK42 14 C2
Knarsdale Wk. MK41 8 D3
Kneller Clo. MK41 7 H6
Knights Av. MK41 6 B1

Laburnum Av. MK40 10 D4
Lacock Abbey. MK41 12 D2
Ladies Wk. MK43 14 A2
Lambourn Way. MK41 7 H4
Lancaster Av. MK42 15 G1
Lancaster Rd. MK42 Inset 16
Lanchester Rd. MK42 6 C2
Landseer Wk. MK41 7 F6
Langdale. MK41 8 A5
Lansdowne Rd. MK40 11 H2
Larkway. MK41 7 H4
Laurel Wk. MK42 14 B2
Lavenham Dri. MK40 10 A2
Lawrence St. MK40 11 F3
Leasway. MK41 8 B5
Lee Clo. MK40 11 H3
Leighfield Clo. MK41 9 E5
Leith Rd. MK42 12 B5
Lely Clo. MK41 7 E7
Leven Wk. MK41 7 G2
Lewes Gdns. MK41 8 C3
Ley Side. MK43 5 D7
Library Wk. MK41 8 B4
Lichfield Clo. MK41 12 D1
Lilac Clo. MK42 14 D2
Lily Clo. MK42 12 B6
Lime Clo. MK43 5 C8
Lime St. MK40 11 F3
Lincoln Rd,
  Harrowden. MK42 Inset 16
Lincoln Rd,
  Kempston. MK42 14 B3
Lincroft. MK43 4 E2

*Linden Ct,
  Linden Rd. MK41 11 E2
Linden Rd. MK41 11 E2
Lindisfarne Priory. MK41 12 D2
Line Wk. MK41 7 G3
Link Way. MK41 8 C5
Linnet Way. MK41 7 G4
Little Grove Pl. MK40 11 G3
Little Headlands. MK41 8 B3
Little Townsend Clo.
  MK42 15 F2
Littledale St. MK42 14 D1
Lodge Av. MK42 14 B3
Lombardy Clo. MK41 8 A4
London Rd. MK42 11 G5
Longholme Way. MK42 11 H4
Longleat. MK41 13 E1
Lorraine Rd. MK43 17 B2
Lovat Wk. MK42 14 D2
Lovell Rd. MK42 12 B5
Lovell Rd. MK43 4 E3
Loveridge Av. MK42 10 B5
Lower Farm Rd. MK43 5 E5
Lowther Rd. MK41 8 A3
Lucas Ct. MK40 10 B2
Ludlow Wk. MK41 8 C4
Luke Pl. MK42 15 G2
Lunedale Clo. MK42 14 C2
Lurke St. MK40 11 G3
Luton Rd. MK42 15 E3
Lydford Clo. MK40 8 B6
Lymington Gdns. MK41 9 E4
Lynn Clo. MK42 15 F1
Lynton Gro. MK42 15 F1
Lyon Clo. MK42 14 C4

Mabel Rd. MK42 11 H6
Magnolia Clo. MK41 14 D3
Main Rd. MK40 10 A3
Maitland St. MK40 11 F3
Makakand Rd. MK42 14 D2
Malcote Clo. MK40 10 A2
Mallard Hill. MK41 7 F5
Malmesbury Abbey.
  MK41 12 C2
Maltings Way. MK44 17 C4
Malvern Av. MK41 8 B5
Manor Clo. MK43 5 E5
Manor Dri. MK42 14 B2
Manor Rd,. MK40 10 A3
Manor Rd. MK41 8 C6
Manor Rd. MK43 17 C2
Manorbier Rd. MK41 8 B3
Manton Centre. MK41 7 E5
Manton La. MK41 7 E6
Mapina Ct. MK42 14 D2
Mardale Clo. MK42 14 D2
Mareth Rd. MK42 14 D1
Margetts Rd. MK42 14 D1
Marigold Way. MK42 12 B6
Mark Rutherford Rd.
  MK42 7 H4
Marlborough Pk. MK42 10 D5
Marlborough Rd. MK40 10 D3
Marlow Way. MK41 7 G2
Marne St. MK42 11 E6
Marshall Clo. MK42 10 B6
Marshall St. MK41 8 C6
Martham Clo. MK40 10 C4
Martin Clo. MK41 7 H4
Maryville Rd. MK42 11 H6
Massey Clo. MK42 14 C2
*Mayes Yd,
  St Pauls Sq. MK40 11 F3
Mayfield Clo. MK40 10 C5
Mayhew Clo. MK43 5 C8
Meadow La. MK40 13 F3
Meadow Vw Rd. MK42 14 B2
Meadowsweet Dri.
  MK42 12 A6
Meadway. MK41 8 C6
Medbury La. MK42 15 G4
Melbourne St. MK41 11 F4
Mendip Cres. MK41 8 B5
Mepham Rd. MK41 17 C1
Merlin Gdns. MK41 7 G4
Mersey Way. MK41 7 G3
Merton Rd. MK40 11 H1
Midland Rd. MK40 11 F3
Milburn Rd. MK41 8 D3
Mile Rd. MK42 15 G1
Mill La. MK42 14 B2
Mill St. MK40 11 G3
Millbrook Rd. MK42 11 F5
Miller Rd. MK42 15 E7
Millfield. MK43 5 D7
Milne Row. MK41 10 D2
Milton Clo. MK41 11 E2
Milton Rd. MK41 6 A1
Mitford Clo. MK41 8 C3
Mitre Clo. MK41 12 D1
Mobbs Clo. MK42 10 B6
Molivers La. MK43 4 D2
Mollymoore Av. MK42 14 B2
Monkshill. MK41 8 C5
Monmouth Clo. MK42 11 H6

Monoux Rd. MK43 17 C3
Moor La. MK42 15 H2
Moriston Rd. MK41 7 G3
Morland Way. MK41 7 F5
Mortimer Rd. MK42 10 B5
Moss La. MK42 15 G4
Moulton Av. MK42 12 A4
Mount Dri. MK41 8 C5
Mount Pleasant Rd. MK41 6 B2
Mountbatten Pl. MK41 12 D1
Mowbray Clo. MK43 5 C6
Mowbray Pl. MK44 16 C1
Mowbray Rd. MK41 8 C5
Mowsbury Wk. MK41 7 G3
*Mulberry Wk,
  Elstow Rd. MK42 14 C2
Murdock Rd. MK41 7 E5
Muswell Rd. MK42 11 F6
Myrtle Rd. MK42 11 H6

Napier Rd. MK41 9 F4
Nash Rd. MK42 12 A4
Naylor Av. MK42 14 C3
Neale Rd. MK43 17 C1
Neale Way. MK43 17 C2
Neath Abbey. MK41 12 D2
Needwood Rd. MK41 8 D4
Nelson St. MK40 11 E4
Nevern Gdns. MK40 10 B2
Neville Clo. MK43 5 C7
Neville Cres. MK43 5 C7
New Rd. MK41 5 C8
New Rd. MK44 17 C6
Newark Av. MK41 8 C3
Newbury Clo. MK41 14 C1
Newnham Av. MK41 12 B2
Newnham Rd. MK41 11 G3
Newnham St. MK41 11 G3
Newstead Way. MK41 8 B3
Newton Rd. MK42 11 G6
Nicholls Rd. MK42 11 H5
Nightingale Av. MK41 7 G4
*Nith Wk,
  Carron Rd. MK41 7 G2
Nodders Way. MK40 10 A3
Norfolk Clo. MK41 7 H2
Norman Clo. MK42 17 B4
Normandy Clo. MK41 11 E6
Norse Rd. MK41 8 D3
North Dri. MK42 Inset 16
North End. MK42 Inset 16
Northampton Rd,
  Bromham. MK43 5 C7
Northampton Rd,
  Thistley Grn. MK43 5 A6
Northcote. MK41 8 C4
Northdale Clo. MK41 15 E1
Nursery Gdns. MK41 8 A4
Nutwood Clo. MK41 8 C4

Oak Clo. MK43 17 C2
Oak Rd. MK42 11 H6
Oaklands Rd. MK41 11 H1
Oakley Clo. MK43 5 E5
Oakley Rd. MK41 6 C2
Odell Clo. MK42 10 C5
Offa Rd. MK41 11 F6
Old Ford End Rd. MK40 10 C4
*Old George Yd,
  Silver St. MK40 11 F3
Old Harrowden Rd.
  MK42 Inset 16
Old Oaks Dri. MK40 10 B3
Oldfield Rd. MK40 10 D4
Ombersley Rd. MK41 11 F5
Orchard Clo. MK43 5 D6
Orchard Clo. MK41 8 A4
Orchard St. MK41 14 C3
Orchard Wk. MK44 17 C5
Ormesby Way. MK40 10 C4
Orwell Clo. MK41 7 G4
Osprey Clo. MK41 14 C3
*Ossory Way,
  Millbrook Rd. MK42 11 F5
Otter Wk. MK41 7 G3
Ouse Rd. MK41 8 C6
Ouseland Rd. MK40 10 D4
Overdale. MK41 8 C4
Owen Clo. MK42 14 B3
*Padbury House,
  Bromham Rd. MK40 10 D2
Paddock Clo. MK41 6 B1
Palmerston St. MK41 11 F1
*Paradine Ct,
  Harpur St. MK0 11 F2
Paradine Rd. MK42 11 H5
Park Av. MK40 11 E2
Park Rd. MK42 14 D1
Park Rd. MK41 7 F6
Park Rd Nth. MK41 11 F2
Park Rd West. MK41 11 F2
Parkland. MK43 5 B6
Parkstone Clo. MK41 8 A2
Parsonage Clo. MK43 Inset 16
Paul Waller Av. MK41 8 A3
Pax Hill. MK41 8 A3

Payne Rd. MK43 17 C3
Pear Tree Vw. MK42 15 G4
Pearcey Rd. MK42 11 G6
Pearmain Clo. MK44 8 B6
Peashill La. MK44 17 B4
*Peel St,
  Tavistock St. MK40 11 F2
Pemberley Av. MK40 11 G1
Pemberley La. MK40 11 G2
Pembroke St. MK40 12 A2
Pendennis Rd. MK41 8 C3
Penlee Clo. MK41 8 B6
Pennine Rise. MK41 8 A5
Pentland Rise. MK41 8 A5
Penwright Clo. MK42 10 C6
Perkins Rd. MK41 9 E6
Pershore Clo. MK41 8 B3
*Petterill Wy,
  Carron Rd. MK41 7 G2
Pevensey Rd. MK41 8 D4
Phillpots Av. MK40 12 B1
*Pilcroft St,
  Ampthill St. MK42 11 G4
Pilgrims Clo. MK42 15 G2
Pilgrims Way. MK42 15 G2
Pinsent Av. MK43 5 C8
Pipit Rise. MK41 7 G5
Plover Way. MK41 7 F4
Polhill Av. MK41 8 A5
Polo Field Way. MK42 14 D4
Popes Rd. MK43 17 B2
Poplar Av. MK41 8 A3
Poppyfields. MK41 9 E4
Portland Clo. MK41 8 C6
Postley Rd. MK42 14 C4
Potters Cross. MK43 17 C2
Poulter Clo. MK40 11 F4
Powis Rd. MK41 8 D3
Prebend St. MK40 11 F3
Prentice Gdns. MK42 10 D6
Preservine Wk. MK41 6 C3
Preston Rd. MK40 10 D3
Princes Rd. MK41 5 C7
Princes St. MK40 11 F2
Princess St. MK41 6 B2
Prinknash Rd. MK41 8 B3
Priory Business
  Centre. MK44 13 E4
Priory St. MK41 11 F3
Proctor Clo. MK42 10 B6
Progress Way. MK42 15 F2
Prudden Clo. MK42 15 F2
Purbeck Clo. MK41 8 C5
Putnoe Heights. MK41 8 B4
Putnoe La. MK41 8 A5
Putnoe St. MK41 8 B3
Pyms Clo. MK44 17 B5

Quantock Clo. MK41 8 B5
Quantrelle Ct. MK42 Inset 16
Queen Alexandra Rd.
  MK41 12 C1
Queen St. MK40 11 F2
Queens Clo. MK40 10 B2
Queens Cres,
  Clapham. MK41 6 B2
Queens Cres,
  Putnoe. MK41 8 B4
Queens Dri. MK41 8 B4
Queensbury Clo. MK40 11 E3
Quenby Way. MK43 5 D8

Race Meadows Way.
  MK42 14 D4
Radnor Wk. MK41 8 D4
Raglan Grn. MK41 8 C3
Railton Rd. MK42 14 C4
Raleigh St. MK40 10 D4
Ram Yd. MK40 11 G3
Ramillies Clo. MK42 11 E6
Ramsay Clo. MK41 7 F6
Ramsey Clo. MK42 14 B4
Randalls Clo. MK43 5 D7
Ranworth Wk. MK40 10 C4
Ravensden Rd. MK41 8 D1
Rays Clo. MK41 11 G4
Reddall Clo. MK42 12 B5
Rede Clo. MK41 7 G3
Redwood Gro. MK42 11 G5
Regent Clo. MK41 7 G2
Regents Mews. MK40 10 B3
*Rendlesham Wk,
  Kershope Clo. MK41 9 E5
Repton Clo. MK42 8 B3
Restormel Clo. MK41 8 B3
Reynes Dri. MK43 4 D2
Reynolds Clo. MK42 7 E6

Ribble Way. MK41 7 G3
Richmond Rd. MK41 11 H2
Ridge Rd. MK43 14 A3
Ridgmount Rd. MK42 11 F5
Ringwood Clo. MK42 15 E2
Ripon Clo. MK42 10 C5
Risborough Rd. MK41 12 B1
River St. MK40 11 F3
River Way. MK42 14 B2
Riverfield Dri. MK41 12 C2
Riverside Clo. MK42 11 E5
*Riverside Sq,
  Batts Ford. MK40 11 F3
Robin Hill. MK41 7 G5
Rockback Clo. MK42 14 D2
Rockingham Wk. MK41 8 D5
Roff Av. MK41 11 F2
Roise St. MK40 11 F3
*Romney Wk, Rowlandson
  Way. MK41 7 E6
Ronald Clo. MK42 14 D4
Rooksmead. MK41 7 G5
Rope Wk. MK42 11 G4
Rosamond Rd. MK40 12 A2
Rose Yd. MK40 11 G3
Roseby Way. MK41 12 C2
Rosedale Way. MK42 14 D2
Rosemary Dri. MK41 5 D7
Rossendale Wk. MK41 8 D4
Rother Clo. MK41 7 H4
Rothsay Gdns. MK40 11 H2
Rothsay Pl. MK40 11 H2
Rothsay Rd. MK40 11 H2
Roundmead. MK41 8 C5
Rowallan Dri. MK41 8 A3
Rowlandson Way. MK41 7 F6
Roxton Rd. MK44 17 B4
Royle Gdns. MK41 12 C5
Ruffs Furze. MK43 4 D2
Rush Ct. MK40 11 G2
Russell Av. MK40 12 A2
Russell Way. MK43 17 B3
Rutland Rd. MK41 11 E3
Ryswick Rd. MK41 11 E6
Ryton Clo. MK41 7 G2

Saddle Clo. MK41 6 B2
Saffron Clo. MK41 11 F3
St Alban Rd. MK40 11 H1
St Andrews Rd. MK40 11 G1
St Augustines Rd. MK40 11 G1
St Cuthberts St. MK40 11 G1
St Edmond Rd. MK40 11 H1
St Georges Rd. MK40 11 H1
St Helena Rd. MK42 11 H6
St Helens Gdns. MK42 15 F2
St Johns Av. MK42 14 C3
St Johns St. MK42 11 G4
St Johns Wk. MK41 14 B3
St Leonards Av. MK42 11 G5
St Leonards St. MK42 11 G5
*St Loyes St,
  Allhallows. MK40 11 F3
St Martins Business
  Centre. MK42 12 D5
St Martins Way. MK42 12 D5
St Marys
  Embankment. MK42 11 F4
St Marys Rd. MK43 17 B2
St Marys St. MK42 11 G3
St Mathews Clo. MK42 14 C3
St Michaels Rd. MK40 11 G1
St Minver Rd. MK40 11 H1
St. Neots Rd. MK41 9 F5
St. Pauls Rd. MK40 10 D4
St. Pauls Sq. MK41 11 F3
St. Peters St. MK40 11 G2
Salcombe Clo. MK40 12 B1
Salisbury St. MK41 7 F6
Saltash Clo. MK41 8 A6
Sanders Clo. MK40 10 B5
Sandhurst Pl. MK41 11 F5
Sandhurst Rd. MK41 11 F5
Sandy Rd. MK41 12 D1
Sandy Rd. MK44 16 C2
Saunders Gdns. MK40 10 D4
Savannah Clo. MK41 11 E6
*Savernake Wk,
  Charnwood Av. MK41 8 D4
Saville Clo. MK44 17 C4
School La. MK41 7 H3
Scott Av. MK42 Inset 16
Seaton Dri. MK41 8 A6
Selsey Clo. MK41 8 A5
Sergeants Way. MK41 9 E5
Severn Way. MK41 7 G3
Sexton Av. MK42 15 E2

Shaftesbury Av. MK40 12 A2
Shakespeare Rd. MK41 11 E1
*Shaldon Ct,
  Barnstaple Rd. MK40 8 A6
Shearley Clo. MK40 10 D4
Sheeplands. MK41 8 D5
Sherbourne Way. MK41 8 B3
Sherwood Wk. MK41 8 D4
Short St. MK40 10 D4
Shuttleworth Rd. MK41 9 E5
*Sibton Abbey, Atherston
  Abbey. MK41 12 D2
Sidney Rd. MK40 10 D2
*Sidmouth Clo,
  Barnstaple Rd. MK40 8 A6
Silver St. MK40 11 F3
Silver St. MK44 17 B5
Silverdale St. MK40 14 D1
Singer Way. MK42 14 C4
*Skerne Passage,
  Carron Rd. MK41 7 G2
Slade Wk. MK41 7 E6
Slater Clo. MK42 10 B6
Somerton Clo. MK41 8 C3
*Somerton Wk,
  Somerton Clo. MK41 8 C3
Sopwith Way. MK42 Inset 16
South Av. MK41 15 G4
South Dri. MK42 Inset 16
Southfields Rd. MK42 15 E2
Southville Rd. MK42 11 F6
Southway. MK42 12 A5
Sovereigns Quay. MK40 11 F5
Spenser Rd. MK40 10 D2
Spring Gdns. MK42 15 E1
Spring Rd. MK42 15 E1
Springfield Av. MK42 14 D2
Springfield Dri. MK43 5 C6
Spruce Wk. MK42 14 D2
Squires Rd. MK43 17 C3
Stafford Rd. MK42 11 E5
Stafford Rd. MK43 4 D1
Stagsden Rd. MK43 5 C8
Stainmore Rd. MK41 9 E4
Stancliffe Rd. MK41 8 A4
Stanhope Rd. MK41 8 A3
Stanley St. MK41 11 F1
Stanley St. MK42 14 D1
Stannard Way. MK44 13 E4
Stanton Rd. MK42 10 C6
Stapleton Rd. MK42 15 H2
Starling Way. MK41 7 G4
Station Rd. MK42 11 G5
Station Rd. MK43 4 E1
Station Rd. MK44 16 C2
Stewart Ct. MK41 8 A5
Stirling Rd. MK42 Inset 16
*Stoke Albany Mews,
  Bromham Rd. MK40 11 E2
Stokesay Clo. MK41 8 C3
Stonedale Rd. MK42 15 E2
Stour Way. MK41 7 G3
Strathconon Way. MK41 9 E4
Stratton Way. MK41 9 E4
Stuart Rd. MK42 14 C2
Studley Rd. MK43 17 B2
Sudeley Wk. MK41 8 C4
Sunbeam Way. MK42 14 C4
*Sunningdale Wk,
  Birkdale Rd. MK41 8 A2
*Swale Path,
  Carron Rd. MK41 7 G2
Swift Clo. MK41 7 F4
Swindale. MK41 7 H3
Symonds Clo. MK43 5 D8

Talbot Rd. MK40 12 A1
Tamar Rd. MK41 7 H3
Tamworth Rd. MK41 8 C3
Tate Clo. MK41 7 F6
Taunton Clo. MK41 8 C3
Tavistock Pl. MK40 11 F2
Tavistock St. MK40 11 F2
Telford Way. MK42 12 D5
Tempsford St. MK42 14 C2
Tennyson Rd. MK40 12 B2
Test Clo. MK41 7 H2
Thackmans Wk. MK42 7 H2
The Alders. MK42 14 C3
The Almonds. MK42 15 E2
The Arcade. MK40 11 F3
The Avenue. MK40 11 E3
The Barn. MK44 13 G5
The Baulk. MK44 6 D2
The Baulk. MK43 11 G3
The Boundary. MK41 8 C5
The Briars. MK42 14 D3

*The Broadway,
  Tavistock St. MK40 11 F2
The Buntings. MK41 7 G5
The Causeway. MK43 14 A2
The Cloisters. MK41 12 D1
The Close. MK41 6 C3
The Close. MK44 17 C5
The Copse. MK41 8 D5
The Crescent. MK40 11 F2
The Crescent. MK41 16 A4
The Crescent. MK42 Inset 16
The Croft. MK41 8 C5
The Dell. MK42 14 A3
The Elms. MK42 14 B3
The Embankment. MK40 11 G3
The Fairway. MK41 8 A2
The Finches. MK40 11 E2
The Firs. MK42 14 D3
The Furlong. MK41 8 B4
*The Gelt
  Carron Rd. MK41 7 G2
The Glen. MK42 14 B2
The Graylings. MK42 8 B4
The Green. MK44 13 F6
The Grove. MK40 11 G2
The Highway. MK41 Inset 16
The Hollies. MK42 14 D3
The Hoo. MK42 14 A3
The Hornbeams. MK42 15 E2
The Larches. MK42 14 D3
*The Limes, Shakespeare
  Rd. MK40 15 E1
The Links. MK42 14 C3
The Maples. MK42 14 C2
The Mews. MK40 11 G2
The Paddock. MK40 10 B2
The Pines. MK42 14 D3
The Planes. MK41 8 C4
The Ridgeway. MK41 8 C4
The Rowans. MK42 14 D3
The Silver Birches. MK42 14 D3
The Slade. MK41 6 C3
The Spencers. MK44 17 C4
The Spinney. MK41 8 D5
The Sycamores. MK42 14 D3
The Warren. MK41 6 C3
The Wear. MK41 7 G2
The Wharf. MK41 7 G2
The Willows. MK43 17 C2
Thirlford Clo. MK42 14 C2
Thirlmere Rd. MK41 7 H2
Thistley Grn. MK43 5 C8
Thistley La. MK43 5 C8
Thomson Av. MK42 Inset 16
Thornton St. MK40 10 D1
Thorpe Clo. MK40 10 A2
Thorpe Way. MK43 17 C2
Threave Clo. MK41 8 B3
Thurlestone Clo. MK40 12 B1
Thurlow Clo. MK41 11 F3
Thurne Way. MK41 7 H2
Tinsley Clo. MK41 6 B1
*Tintagel Wk,
  Dover Cres. MK41 8 C3
Tintern Abbey. MK41 12 D2
Tipcat Clo. MK42 15 F2
Tithe Barn Rd. MK43 17 B3
Tiverton Rd. MK40 11 H2
Tollgate Clo. MK43 5 C8
Top End. MK41 9 G1
Torre Abbey. MK41 12 D2
Torridge Rise. MK41 7 G3
Totnes Rd. MK40 12 B1
Trent Rd. MK41 7 H3
Trevor Dri. MK43 5 C7
Trevor St. MK40 11 E2
Trinity Rd. MK40 10 D4
Triumph Way. MK42 14 C4
Troon Clo. MK41 8 A2
Tudor Clo. MK41 11 E2
Tudor Clo. MK43 5 D6
*Tunstall Wk,
  Kershope Clo. MK41 9 E5
*Turnberry Wk,
  Birkdale Rd. MK41 8 A2
Turner Way. MK41 7 F6
Turnpike West. MK41 8 D5
Tweedsmuir Rd. MK41 8 B3
Twinwood Rd. MK41 6 B1
Tyne Cres. MK41 7 G3

Ullswater Clo. MK42 14 C2
Union St. MK40 11 F2
Uplands. MK41 8 B4

Vanguard Clo. MK42 10 C5
Vicars Clo. MK40 10 A3

Vicars Wk. MK41 8
Victoria Rd. MK42 11
Viking Gro. MK42 10
Viking Ind Est. MK41 9
Village Rd. MK43 17
Vineyard Way. MK42 12
Violet Clo. MK42 12
Vulcan St. MK42 10
Vyne Clo. MK42 10

Wagstaffe Clo. MK41 8 A
Walcourt Rd. MK41 8 C5
Walnut Wk. MK42 14
Waltham Clo. MK41 8
Wansbeck Rd. MK41 7 H
Warren Abbey. MK41 12
Warwick Av. MK40 11
Warwick Ho. MK41 11
Washburn Clo. MK41 7
Water End. MK44 16 A
Water La. MK41 8
Waterloo Rd. MK41 11 C
Waveney Av. MK41 7 H
Weaver Clo. MK41 7 H
Webbs Clo. MK43 17 F
Wedgwood Rd. MK41 7 F
Welbeck Gdns. MK41 8
Welbourne Gdns. MK42 12
Wellington Rd. MK42 Inset
Wellington St. MK40 11 F
Wells Clo. MK42 14
Wendover Dri. MK41 12 E
Wenlock Rd. MK42 14 E
Wensum Wk. MK41 7 H
Wentworth Dri. MK41 8
*West Arcade,
  Harpur St. MK40 11 F
West End. MK42 11
West Gro. MK40 10 D
Westbourne Rd. MK40 11 F
Westdale Wk. MK42 15 E
Western St. MK40 11 F
Westfield Rd. MK40 10 D
Westfield Rd. MK43 10 C
Westminster Gdns. MK42 10 C
Westrope Way. MK41 8
Westwood Clo. MK41 Inset
Wheathouse Clo. MK41 8 B
Whitbread Av. MK42 11 E
White Lodge Clo. MK42 14 C
Whitebeam Clo. MK42 14 C
Whitley Rd. MK42 Inset
Whittingstall Av. MK42 15 E
Widecombe Clo. MK40 12 B
Wigram Clo. MK42 15 F
Wilden Rd. MK41 9 E
Wildflower Way. MK42 12 E
*Williamson Ct,
  Williamson Rd. MK42 14 E
Williamson Rd. MK42 14 E
Willington Rd. MK44 16 A
Willoughby Clo. MK44 17 B
Willow Rd. MK42 11 H
Willsher Wk. MK42 11
Wilmers Clo. MK41 6 B
Wilstead Rd. MK42 15 G
Winchester Rd. MK42 12 B
Windmill Clo. MK41 8 B
Windmill Hill. MK40 10 B
Windrush Av. MK41 7 H
Windsor Gdns. MK40 10 D
Windsor Rd. MK42 15 H
Wingfield Clo. MK40 10 C
Wingfield Rd. MK43 14 A
Winifred Rd. MK40 10 D
Witham Clo. MK41 7 H
Woburn Ct. MK42 14
Woburn Rd. MK40 11 E
Woburn Rd. MK42 14 B
Woburn Rd Ind Est.
  MK42 14 C
Wolseley Rd. MK41 8
Wood Clo. MK40 10 B
Wood La. MK41 9 G
Wood La. MK44 16 C
Woodcote. MK41 8 B
Woodland Dri. MK43 17 C
Woodlands Clo. MK44 16 A
Woodmere. MK41 8 B
Woodstock Rd. MK41 11 C
Worcester Rd. MK42 12 B
Wroxham Way. MK40 10 B
Wyatt Rd. MK41 14 B
Wychwood Rd. MK41 8 D
Wye Clo. MK41 7 H

Yeomans Gate. MK44 13 F
York St. MK40 12